Old DEAN and STOCKBRID

by
Malcolm Cant

This sylvan scene showing St Bernard's Bridge comes from *Modern Athens* by Thomas H. Shepherd, published in 1831, a year before the Dean Bridge was opened. St Bernard's Bridge was constructed in 1824 with a single span crossing the Water of Leith and a smaller arch (seen to the right) providing access along the riverbank. A substantial flight of steps with heavy balustrades was added in 1887, giving access to the riverside walk which passes St Bernard's Well (see page 48) a few hundred yards upstream from the bridge.

ACKNOWLEDGEMENTS

This short illustrated history of the communities of Dean and Stockbridge is the fourth book I have written as part of Stenlake Publishing's 'bygone' series, and as always I have enjoyed the task. In doing so I acknowledge again the assistance of many people who have provided me with information for the captions or helped locate suitable material for the book. Specific pictures have been acknowledged in the captions.

This rather uninspiring sketch of Ross's Folly belies an interesting history. It stood in the grounds of the former St Bernard's House, near present-day Dean Terrace, which was owned by the humorous and eccentric Walter Ross, WS. In an effort to reduce vandalism on his property, he acquired a human leg from the Royal Infirmary, dressed it up in a stocking, shoe and buckle, and sent it round the village of Stockbridge with the town crier, who held it aloft, proclaiming that it had been found in a man-trap in the grounds of St Bernard's House the previous night, and offering to restore it to anyone who could make up the matching pair. Walter Ross's crowning achievement was undoubtedly his own folly, erected on the highest point of the north-west corner of the estate. It was about forty feet high and twenty feet square, consisting of two rooms, one above the other, the upper one being reached by an outside stairway which wound round three sides of the tower. When Ross died suddenly and mysteriously on 11 March 1789 his body was interred in the lower storey of the tower with the lid of the coffin left open. In 1818, when the surrounding area was being redeveloped, Ross's remains were reinterred in St Cuthbert's Churchyard at the West End of Edinburgh.

INTRODUCTION

The old villages of Dean and Stockbridge have been distinct communities for a very long time, and remain quite separate districts of Edinburgh, albeit hemmed in on all sides by the greater conurbation. As the crow flies, or perhaps more appropriately as the Water of Leith flows, the two villages are not far apart. On the Water of Leith Walkway, at a point between St Bernard's Well (nearest to Stockbridge) and St George's Well (nearest to Dean) the two communities are only a few hundred yards apart.

Dean is the older of the two communities. Its history can be traced back to the time of King David I through association with the Ancient Incorporation of Baxters (bakers), who conferred the profits of the village's mills on the abbot and canons regular of St Augustine at Holyrood. At one time there were two separate communities with rather similar names, which has caused confusion over the years. The present Dean Village, below Telford's Dean Bridge, was once known as Water of Leith Village, whereas Village of Dean was the name given to a separate, much smaller community, on the north side of the river near the gates to Dean Cemetery. Village of Dean consisted of one main street with two or three minor lanes running off it to the east. For the most part, the houses were small and single-storeyed with thatched roofs, but there were other larger dwellings of two storeys, the upper floors being reached by an outside stair. The village's inhabitants were mostly carters and quarrymen at Craigleith Quarry, or employed at Dean Farm or Dean House, which stood on the site of present-day Dean Cemetery. As early as 1743 Village of Dean had a population of almost 400, which was adequate to support the main aspects of village life, for example, a shoemaker, smithy, cartwright, and Mrs Burr's hostelry.

Water of Leith Village, in the hollow, became what is known today as Dean Village. It was much larger and contained a school, church, several hostelries and numerous mills which derived their power from the Water of Leith. The village formed an enduring association with the ancient trades of baxters (bakers) and weavers. Even today, although the mill wheels no longer turn, several old industrial buildings and their inscriptions bear witness to this important era. The existence of mills and granaries at Dean can be traced to the twelfth century, their importance to the community being jealously guarded by the Ancient Incorporation of Baxters. The incorporation's influence in matters of employment and the local economy found expression in the annual Feeing of the Millers, at which the hiring of labour and settling of wages took place. After the formal business was completed, the day was not without its moments of relaxation and indulgence if the old accounts of expenditure are anything to go by. Listed after the main items in the accounts for beef, veal, broth, bread, ale and brandy there are two additions – for more ale and more brandy.

Today Dean Village is among Edinburgh's most attractive locations, with an interesting range of houses and small businesses located in buildings of widely differing ages and architectural styles.

Stockbridge is Edinburgh's New Town village and straddles the Water of Leith between the older communities of Dean, to the west, and Canonmills, to the east. Although Stockbridge cannot claim great antiquity, its two centuries of recorded history provide abundant evidence of its contribution to the history and character of Edinburgh. Its principal claim to fame in earlier years was undoubtedly the long list of artists, historians and men and women of letters who were either born in the village or lived there at a significant time in their careers. In the early nineteenth century its proximity to the New Town, combined with plenty of space, made it a popular area in which to establish some of the great educational institutions of the day, notably The Edinburgh Academy. The later Victorian era brought the Colonies, tenement buildings, board schools and public transport in the form of cable cars.

The small district of Silvermills, to the south of Henderson Row, now forms part of Stockbridge, but it is much older and its history can be traced to the sixteenth century. It takes its name from the time when ore from a small silver mine at Linlithgow was brought to the village for refining. After a long period of neglect in recent years, Silvermills has again attracted new development and the renovation of some of its older properties. The jewel in the crown is undoubtedly Silvermills House (in West Silvermills Lane), dating from 1760, in which the artist brothers, Robert Scott Lauder (1803–69) and James Eckford Lauder (1811–69) were born.

Modern Stockbridge has the bustle and confidence of a prosperous community of fashionable housing, restaurants, shops and businesses, sitting side by side with some of the earliest relics of the old village.

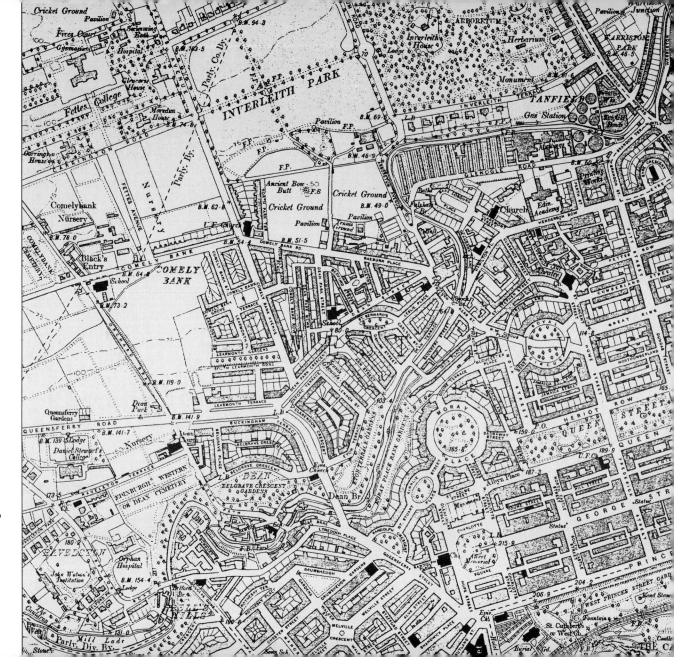

Ordnance Survey map of Dean and Stockbridge (revised 1905–6). *Reproduced by permission of the Trustees of the National Library of Scotland.*

4

This early twentieth century postcard view looks north-west across the Dean Bridge. The church on the far side of the bridge was built in 1838 to designs by John Henderson for the Scottish Episcopal Church. For more than a century Holy Trinity was the home of the city's largest Episcopal congregation, but by 1942 numbers had reduced considerably. At the end of the Second World War the building was used for a while by the German Church, and in the mid-1950s it was sold to the South of Scotland Electricity Board which took the unusual step of using it to house a sub-station serving the West End of Edinburgh. In recent years the sub-station has been resited and the building is again being used as a place of worship. The substantial structure on the left with the crow-stepped gables is Kirkbrae House, dating from the seventeenth century. It was embellished and extended by James Graham Fairley in 1892 as the residence and office of James Stewart, a prosperous cab-hirer.

The Cramond Road Trustees agreed to contribute to the cost of building the Dean Bridge on condition that there would be no toll, and that its design would be approved by Thomas Telford (although in the end it was Telford himself who designed it). Work started in October 1829, and after significant alterations to the plans to increase the number of arches from three to four, the project was completed in December 1831. When the bridge opened in 1832 it was described as a 'stupendous structure which forms one of the most splendid monuments in the city'. As far as Telford was concerned it was certainly a splendid monument, which greatly enhanced his reputation as a bridge builder, but for John Learmonth, Lord Provost of Edinburgh, who owned the ground on its north side, it remained a monument for much longer than his financial predictions had allowed. He had to wait for upwards of twenty years before the tide of building work turned again towards further expansion of the New Town, with the first of the houses being built on his land in Clarendon Crescent in the 1850s. In this view all four arches are evident, with the houses and mills of Dean Village on the right and the rear of the houses in Moray Place, Ainslie Place and Randolph Crescent on the skyline. The dome is that of St George's Parish Church in Charlotte Square, now occupied by the National Archives of Scotland as West Register House.

Today the Dean Bridge carries a volume of traffic which Telford could never have envisaged, nor even imagined, when it was opened in 1832, yet the structure remains in excellent condition. This, of course, is partly due to frequent maintenance checks both externally and internally. Access to the inside of the bridge is by a small manhole on the west pavement. Once inside, it is possible to walk along the length of the bridge by following its curved arches. This photograph was taken in 1985 during one of the maintenance checks. The engineer on the left is about to crawl into the space in the stonework providing access under the carriageway, from where the inspection will continue on the other side.

This small iron pedestrian bridge was erected by Tynecastle Ironworks in 1889. The original ford across the Water of Leith lies between the bridge and the high wall topped by the railings on the right. Today the cobbled slope leading down from each bank is still clearly visible. The large building in the top right-hand corner is Well Court, while that to the right of the bracketed street lamp is part of the premises of Robert Legget & Sons, tanners, who operated in the village for more than a century. The initial treatment of the skins exuded a pungent odour which permeated every corner of the village. Sheepskins were brought in from the slaughterhouses of Aberdeen, Dundee and Edinburgh, the wool being plucked by hand and despatched to the hosiery trade, while the treated skins were later sold to bookbinders and manufacturers of various leather goods. The tenement block in the left-hand corner is Convening Court.

The small, single-span Bell's Brae Bridge carried the main road from the West End of Edinburgh to South Queensferry for more than a century before the opening of the Dean Bridge in 1832. The Bell's Brae route to South Queensferry was not an easy one for heavily-laden horse-drawn wagons. The descent from Queensferry Street was very steep and the ascent on the north side of the Water of Leith was equally difficult, requiring the assistance of trace horses which were stabled in the village. Several of the Dean's important buildings are shown in this general view. Immediately to the left of Bell's Brae is Dean Primary School, designed by the Edinburgh School Board architect, Robert Wilson, and opened in 1875. The school closed in 1961 when the roll had reduced to only 37 pupils. The building on the extreme left, partly hidden by trees, is Well Court, with its clock tower and oriel windows overlooking the Water of Leith. The development was conceived by John Ritchie Findlay, philanthropic owner of *The Scotsman* newspaper, who had it built in 1884 as an experiment in model housing for working people. The architect was Sydney Mitchell, who designed it to be seen from Mr Findlay's house in Rothesay Terrace on the high ground to the south of the village. The half-timbered, yellow-ochre Hawthorn Buildings are on the right, and the pinnacled tower of the former Holy Trinity Church can be seen on the skyline.

Belford Bridge was opened on 22 July 1887 by the Rt. Hon. Sir Thomas Clark, Lord Provost of Edinburgh. On the castellated south parapet (seen on the right) there is a plaque stating that the bridge was erected by Edinburgh Town Council with the aid of local subscriptions obtained by the Belford Bridge Association. The engineers were Cunningham, Blyth & Westland, and the contractors were Henderson, Matthew & Co. The 1887 bridge replaced an earlier one built in 1784, described in one report as 'a tall, narrow, starved, consumptive object unable to support even its own feebleness without the awkward assistance of buttress crutches, in addition to the original plan: it must stand (while it is able to stand) a spectacle of studied deformity'. In complete contrast is the elegant tower and spire of the former Dean Free Church. This was built in 1889, renamed Belford Church in 1929, and is now in secular use. On the left of the picture are the premises of Liddle & Johnston, carriage builders.

This ancient mansion, Dean House, lay to the west of Dean Village in extensive grounds, now laid out as Dean Cemetery. The building displayed every conceivable example of Scottish vernacular architecture, with a variety of turrets, corbels and crow-stepped gables. Internally, there was a great hall, the ceiling of which was decorated with a series of wooden panels painted in oil and tempera. Seven of these panels, some of which depict biblical scenes, were displayed in the Museum of Antiquities in Queen Street, Edinburgh, before being rehoused in the new Museum of Scotland in Chambers Street. For many generations Dean House was the seat of the Nisbet family, William Nisbet of Dean, Lord Provost of Edinburgh, being knighted by James VI when he visited Edinburgh in 1617. When the house was demolished in 1845 many of the carved stones were preserved in a wall in Dean Cemetery, and on Kirkbrae House at the south end of the Dean Bridge.

Dean Orphan Hospital was built on ground adjacent to the former Dean House (demolished for the construction of Dean Cemetery). The hospital was built between 1831 and 1833 from plans drawn up by architect Thomas Hamilton, who also designed the former Royal High School in Regent Road. For over a decade, from 1833 to 1845, the new orphanage and old Dean House must have created quite a spectacular contrast in architecture. After the orphanage was closed the building was used for a variety of purposes, and in recent years housed Dean Education Centre. In 1995, however, elaborate plans were announced for the conversion of the building into an art gallery housing the works of Leith-born sculptor Eduardo Paolozzi. On completion of the gallery new access was created from its grounds to the adjacent Dean Cemetery, which also contains many fine examples of sculpture.

Taken from Dean Bridge and looking north-east, this photograph shows the Water of Leith on the right and the grass and shrubberies of Eton Terrace Gardens (now Dean Gardens) on two levels to the left. Eton Terrace (top left) dates from 1855, with some houses designed by the architects Peddie & Kinnear. The original intention was to use the name Cambridge Terrace to complement the adjacent Oxford Terrace. Of the two small buildings clinging to the right-hand bank of the Water of Leith, the one nearest the camera is St George's Well, which is fronted by a pedimented gable bearing the date 1810 and has a rounded gable-end to the rear, built high above the water's edge. The second building, further downstream, is the much grander St Bernard's Well. Its base is constructed of very large rough-hewn stones, supporting a circular, domed temple of ten plain Doric columns, within which stands a statue of Hygeia.

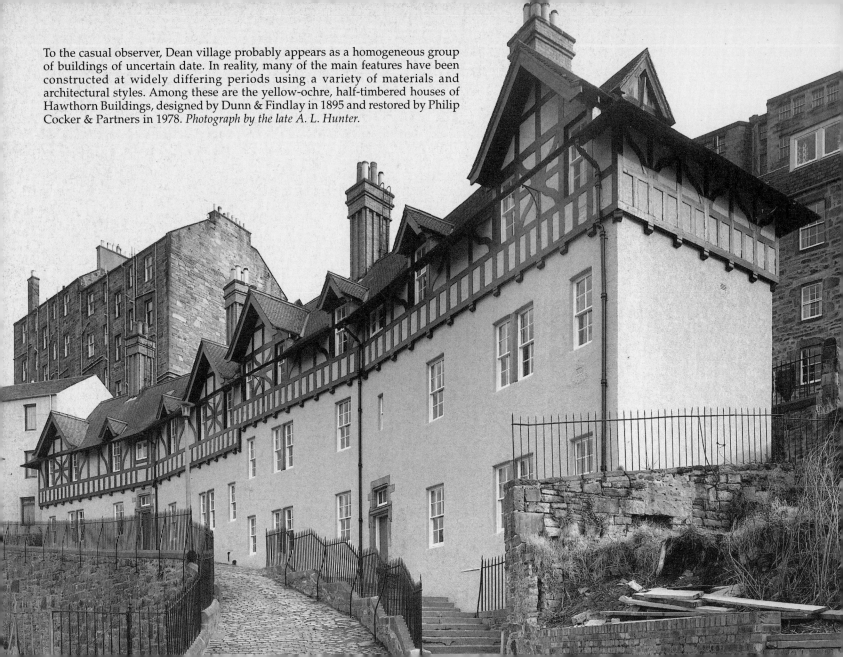

To the casual observer, Dean village probably appears as a homogeneous group of buildings of uncertain date. In reality, many of the main features have been constructed at widely differing periods using a variety of materials and architectural styles. Among these are the yellow-ochre, half-timbered houses of Hawthorn Buildings, designed by Dunn & Findlay in 1895 and restored by Philip Cocker & Partners in 1978. *Photograph by the late A. L. Hunter.*

Dean Village occupies the lower half of this 1993 aerial photograph, with Dean Bridge on the extreme left. The upper half includes most of the western New Town, with the West End at the top left-hand corner. Most of the main buildings of the Dean are visible, although they take on a slightly different appearance from the air. From left to right are: the former Holy Trinity Church at the north end of Dean Bridge; the twin, pitched roofs of West Mill; above, the large-windowed gable of Drumsheugh Baths; Dean Primary School, now converted into flats; the curved frontage of Hawthorn Buildings; and the quadrangle of Well Court. The modern complex of light-coloured flats to the right of Hawthorn Buildings was developed between 1990 and 1992 to designs by Yeoman McAllister on ground previously known as High Green. *Crown copyright: Royal Commission on the Ancient and Historical Monuments of Scotland.*

This view was taken in the same area as the picture featured on the front cover, but at a later date and looking in the opposite direction, towards North West Circus Place. It is typical of one of Edinburgh's main thoroughfares in the late 1950s and early 1960s. The tramway system has gone; the main junction is controlled by traffic lights, rather than a policeman; and parking is becoming a problem before the introduction of meters. Baird the Bootmaker had several branches throughout Edinburgh, including Stockbridge, South Bridge, Home Street, Dalry Road, Morningside Road and Great Junction Street. The corner premises of the Edinburgh Savings Bank with the clock tower dates from 1840, but was extensively remodelled by architects McGibbon & Ross in 1900 to include the balustrade and clock tower. At the same time the interior was redesigned by the famous firm of cabinetmakers, Scott Morton & Co. of Tynecastle, who undertook many similar contracts for banks and insurance companies. The Edinburgh Savings Bank became the Trustee Savings Bank and then Lloyds TSB Scotland, who have since vacated this building.

This section of the Water of Leith Walkway lies between the Stock Bridge, first erected in 1786, and the Falshaw Bridge, built further downstream in 1877. At the Stock Bridge a plaque erected in 1981 denotes the Deanhaugh Path section of the walkway, while at the Falshaw Bridge there is another plaque stating that this section was opened by Lord Provost Tom Morgan on 18 February the same year. Over the last twenty years substantial progress has been made in creating a continuous walkway along the banks of the Water of Leith from Balerno to Leith. The headquarters and visitors' centre for the Water of Leith Conservation Trust is at Lanark Road in Slateford.

For many years the local fire station and police station in Hamilton Place were a conspicuous part of the old village of Stockbridge. The informal group on the left is standing outside the fire station, typical of similar structures built in Edinburgh at Abbeyhill, Braid Place (now Sciennes House Place) and Angle Park Terrace. The Hamilton Place fire station was later relocated to Saunders Street, after which its predecessor in Stockbridge was turned into a public toilet. The two police officers on the right of the picture are standing outside Stockbridge police station, which is considerably more modest than its counterpart in Braid Place or Abbeyhill. It currently houses a fashionable restaurant. *Courtesy of Lothian & Borders Fire Brigade.*

Stockbridge fire brigade, in formal pose, seen outside the station in Hamilton Place *c.*1900, when brass helmets, buttons and accoutrements were the order of the day. The actual fire-fighting equipment was, however, rather rudimentary and not very speedy. Curiously, the building's lamp is positioned near the ridge of the roof and has an access board fitted to the slates, while in the picture on the facing page the lamp appears in the more typical position above the door. *Courtesy of Lothian & Borders Fire Brigade.*

Situated in Hamilton Place, Stockbridge Public School was designed in the Gothic style in 1874 by R. Rowand Anderson as one of the earliest board schools. It was intended to cater for 600 pupils, most of whom lived locally and had formerly attended St Bernard's Free Church School, St Mary's Public School or Deanhaugh Street School. Stockbridge Public School was opened on 12 January 1877 with a roll of 537 children and a large crowd of parents and friends in attendance. The dignitaries included Professor Calderwood of the Edinburgh School Board and several bailies and councillors representing the city. As the school settled down, activities were organised according to children's ability, rather than their age. Not everything ran smoothly though, and it is recorded that the janitor was sent out 'to locate truanters, many of whom were beyond all control of parents'.

When this view of West Claremont Street was captured c.1910 it was free of parked cars, had gas street lighting, and a house was for sale on the right (with another to let nearer the church). In 1968 West Claremont Street was renamed Saxe Coburg Street to avoid confusion with East Claremont Street in Broughton. The building on the right with the clock tower and pedimented frontage was designed by James Milne and opened on 16 November 1823 as West Claremont Street Chapel of Ease. It became a parish church in 1834 and changed its name to St Bernard's Parish Church in 1851, then St Bernard's Stockbridge in 1980. Perhaps its most famous minister was the Revd George Matheson, the 'Blind Seer' who wrote many hymns and books. In 1992 the congregation of St Bernard's Stockbridge and St Stephen's amalgamated to form Stockbridge Parish Church.

Stockbridge School and the janitor's house again appear in this picture, but the centre of attention has shifted to the large informal group which has turned out to watch the street photographer. The picture was taken in Henderson Row looking west to Hamilton Place, with the entrance to Clarence Street on the left and West Claremont Street (now Saxe Coburg Street) on the right. The west side of West Claremont Street, built between 1870 and 1876, was at one time named Deanbank Terrace. A street sign confirming this can just be seen, at first floor level, to the right of the corner shop occupied by John McGowan, grocer and wine merchant.

The St Stephens Motor & Cycle Depot at No. 10 Hamilton Place was operated for many years by the Nelson family, and offered a wide range of accessories and spare parts. *Courtesy of I. McMurtrie.*

Stockbridge Public Baths, Edinburgh.

Stockbridge or Glenogle Public Baths, situated in Glenogle Road (originally Water Lane), were designed by city architect Robert Morham and built between 1897 and 1900. The site was rather awkward to develop, partly on account of the steeply sloping ground, and the (perceived) need to match the classical frontages of nearby Saxe Coburg Place. Even though the fourth buttressed tower was omitted from its intended position nearest to Saxe Coburg Place, the two styles of architecture did not make an ideal marriage. Robert Morham was also the architect of several other public baths in Edinburgh, notably those at Dalry, built between 1893 and 1895.

The rear facade of Glenogle Baths incorporated this pedimented doorway in grey ashlar in an attempt to marry the Gothic architecture of the main building – in red sandstone – to the classical lines of nearby Saxe Coburg Place.

The Stockbridge Colonies lie to the north of Glenogle Road and were built on land shown on Kirkwood's map of 1817 as belonging to J. Stein Esq. Constructed from 1861 onwards by the Edinburgh Co-operative Building Company Ltd., the houses were designed to provide low-priced accommodation for working people. The names of the various terraces commemorate the principal participants in the original company: Hugh Miller, stonemason, journalist and geologist; Hugh Gilzean Reid, journalist, geologist and later Liberal MP; and James Colville, stonemason and first manager of the Co-operative. The addresses of the houses are based on the names of each of the terraces, with the 'high doors' and 'low doors' reached from opposite sides of each block. In this photograph, the steps provide access to the high doors of these two terraces. *Photograph by Phil Seale.*

Rustic Bridge, Glenogle Road, Edinburgh.

This photograph was taken across the river from the north side of the Colonies, where the Rustic Bridge crosses the Water of Leith almost opposite Bell Place. David Bell was a joiner to trade who was elected chairman of the Edinburgh Co-operative Building Company from 1867–9. According to the excellent history of the district, *The Colonies of Stockbridge*, by Rosemary J. Pipes, the bridge was built by John Morris & Sons in 1894 at a total cost of £453 13s.

Arboretum Avenue is the curved section of roadway seen on the left here branching off from St Bernard's Row. The avenue originally formed the southern section of a very long driveway to Inverleith House, which nowadays stands in the grounds of the Royal Botanic Garden. On Kirkwood's map of 1817 the southern section of the driveway is shown as straight and tree-lined. Where it reaches the spot where the west end of present-day Inverleith Terrace lies, the map shows the driveway reducing in width and meandering in a north-easterly direction to Inverleith House and its adjacent stable block. The lodge house on the right of the picture is shown on the 1817 map as a rectangle. Presumably the distance between the gate pillars has been increased over the years in response to road widening.

The pillars at No. 54 Henderson Terrace originally formed the entrance to the Royal Edinburgh Institution for the Deaf and Dumb. In July 1968 the rather plain stonework was greatly enhanced by the addition of ornamental finials and an 'iron' over-gate bearing the inscription 'Marcia Blaine School for Girls' for the filming of *The Prime of Miss Jean Brodie*. Although the film was based around Muriel Spark's recollections of James Gillespie's High School for Girls in Warrender Park Crescent, much of the filming was done in Stockbridge. The street furniture was temporarily altered and the television aerials on the roofs of nearby houses were removed until filming was completed.

The postcard from which this illustration has been reproduced bears the message 'Got this card from Teacher at School on 6.3.18'. Established in 1810, the Royal Edinburgh Institution for the Deaf and Dumb opened this new building, designed by James Gillespie Graham and situated in Henderson Row, in 1823. The foundation stone was laid by one of the senior pupils on 22 May that year in the silent company of his classmates, 'whose looks bespoke the feelings of their minds, and which would have been a sufficient recompense to the contributors for the building, had they been witnesses to the scene'. In 1939 the institution combined with Donaldson's Hospital at West Coates to form Donaldson's School for the Deaf, with senior pupils being taught at West Coates and junior ones at Stockbridge. The younger pupils were transferred to West Coates in 1977, and the Henderson Row building was then sold to The Edinburgh Academy.

At the beginning of the nineteenth century, classical education in Edinburgh was mainly in the hands of the town council's own High School, but several factors were conspiring in favour of a new classical school in the New Town. The vision and drive for this came from two former pupils of the High School, namely Henry Cockburn (later Lord Cockburn) and Leonard Horner, who with John Russell and others brought their plans to fruition in only two years. A site was chosen in Henderson Row and The Edinburgh Academy, designed by the architect William Burn within a budget of £9,000, was opened on 1 October 1824. The initial enrolment of 372 boys sat through lengthy opening orations by Sir Walter Scott and Henry Mackenzie, author of *The Man of Feeling* and other works.

A small boy, perhaps on his way to another school, perches on the wall to the left of the street orderly's cart and brush. He is obviously greatly taken by the display of semaphore being enacted by the academy boys on the school playground, or Front Yards, as the area is known. The instructor can just be seen in front of the right-hand pillar, while the figure to his right appears to be the janitor, dressed in top hat and tails. *Courtesy of The Edinburgh Academy.*

The Hailes Game is described by Magnus Magnusson in *The Clachan and the Slate, the Story of The Edinburgh Academy 1824–1974* as a cross between the Eton Wall Game and shinty: it is seen here in full swing on the academy's Front Yards. The hollow rubber ball is struck with the clachan, an object resembling a large wooden spoon. In this case a special match is featured – Academy v Academicals – held in 1974 to celebrate the 150th anniversary of the school, with, centre right, Gordon Honeycombe, the author and former television newscaster, enjoying every moment. *Courtesy of The Edinburgh Academy.*

HM Queen Elizabeth II visited The Edinburgh Academy at the time of the school's 150th anniversary. In this photograph, taken at Henderson Row on 5 July 1974, Her Majesty is accompanied by Dr H. H. Mills, MC, the rector at the time, and David Gregson, head ephor. *Courtesy of The Edinburgh Academy.*

Situated at the north end of St Vincent Street, St Stephen's Church was designed by William H. Playfair and built between 1827 and 1828. The site was difficult to develop as the ground fell away steeply to the north. This meant that the imposing south doorway, at the head of a huge flight of steps, entered the church at gallery level, while entry to the main body of the building was by two comparatively modest side doors. The tower is 162 feet in height and is said to have contained, when first built, the longest pendulum in Europe. Though generally considered to have met most of the challenges of this awkward site, the absence of lateral support on each side of the yawning entrance prompted Professor Blackie to voice the opinion that it was like 'a mouth without cheeks'. In the mid-1950s extensive reorganisation of the interior divided the church laterally at gallery level so that all the body of the new church was reached from the main entrance. Today the building is in secular use. To the left of St Stephen's is the much smaller St Vincent's Episcopal Church, built in 1857.

N.A.C.B. PICNIC TO BLACKNESS CASTLE AUG 2ND 1919.

Members of the Navy & Army Canteen Board, plus a few onlookers, photographed on the steps of St Stephen's Church on 2 August 1919, before going on their annual picnic to Blackness Castle. The scroll masonry on either side of the main flight of steps is unmistakably the design of the architect William H. Playfair.

In 1985 the north-east section of St Stephen Street was dominated by Cinderellas Rockerfellas, a cacophonous mecca of the young at heart. After a serious fire the building lay empty for many years, and was then replaced by housing, exactly in keeping with the adjacent New Town facade, a small section of which can be seen on the left of the picture. Prior to the 1980s the building had a variety of uses: it opened as the Tivoli Theatre in 1901, became the Grand Theatre in 1904, was then used as a riding academy, and became the Grand Picture House in 1920, remaining so until 1960.

Spring Gardens was at one time the name for this short section of the main road, seen here from North West Circus Place. The name was later abandoned to avoid confusion with Spring Gardens in Abbeyhill. The busy thoroughfare, photographed c.1913 with cable cars heading to and from town, leads northwards to two of Stockbridge's important buildings. On the left is Stockbridge Church, the shell of which was moved in 1868 from its original position on Lothian Road when the Caledonian Railway required more space for development there. The tower and spire were added later at Stockbridge, and, ironically, are all that remain of the church building today. The smaller tower with the clock in the centre of the picture was occupied by the Edinburgh Savings Bank. On the left is the entrance into Church Street, which took its name from Kirk Loan, the road which ran from St Cuthbert's Parish Church at the West End to Stockbridge. Church Street became Gloucester Street in 1966.

This view of Stockbridge was taken a few hundred yards south of the one featured on the facing page, and shows St Stephen Street on the right and India Place to the left. The western section of St Stephen Street was originally named Brunswick Street and gave access to Market Place (now St Stephen Place), appropriately named as the short approach to the former Stockbridge Market. This was designed in 1824 by Archibald Scott to include stalls for fish, poultry, fruit and vegetables; today only the building's stone arch survives. On the right of the picture, the three brass balls protruding from the corner of the tenement denote the Equitable Loan Company, which was established in 1845. Cochrane's Drapery House is on the north corner of St Stephen Street, and Hardie Bros., clothiers & hatters, are on the left of the picture.

A large crowd has gathered at the junction of St Stephen Street and North West Circus Place to watch the local fire brigade tackle a blaze above the premises of Alexander Breck, hatter, at No. 4 Baker's Place, and Robert Bowie, licensed grocer, at No. 5 (below the ladder) in 1901. The fire was a very extensive one which originated in Todd's Flour Mill to the rear of Baker's Place. Several people lost their lives and many others were injured. At the time of writing, Baker's Place forms part of Kerr Street. The tenement buildings on the other side of Kerr Street were demolished many years ago. *Courtesy of Lothian & Borders Fire Brigade.*

Here, North West Circus Place has been transformed into the age of elegance with the help of some careful embellishment. Although the scene looks entirely natural, picture postcards were often enhanced in the studio by the addition of sophisticated ladies and gentlemen, some of whom are seen here apparently strolling the streets of Stockbridge. Even night-time scenes were frequently 'improved' by the addition of the moon – sometimes situated in the *northern* hemisphere if that is what suited the location.

North West Circus Place, Edinburgh.

An open-topped cable car is coming down the steep slope of North West Circus Place, passing, on its left, a line of horse-drawn carriages. The shop on the right of the picture is Alexander Rae's family grocer, wine and spirit merchant at Nos. 2&3 Spring Gardens. Rae's also had premises at 75 Lauriston Street and 30 Newington Road. On the left, the mortar and pestle is situated above the chemist's shop run by John Robertson. Nearer pavement level, a sign appears to read 'shampooing saloon'.

A cable car (advertising Bovril) crosses the single-arch stone bridge which spans the Water of Leith in the centre of Stockbridge. In 1784 local landowners petitioned the trustees of the bridges and highways in the County of Edinburgh, demanding that a bridge be built across the Water of Leith, as a result of which the first structure was erected in 1786. It was a stone bridge of one arch, raised in the centre, which was later levelled and widened *c*.1830. The bridge seen in the picture, which is still in use, has a plaque on each parapet confirming that it was again widened and improved in 1900–01 by the engineer David C. Proudfoot. Dean Terrace, behind the trees on the left of the picture, dates from 1823.

The narrow thoroughfare to the left is Dean Street, while its wider neighbour to the right is Raeburn Place, leading to Comely Bank. Over the years Dean Street has housed a number of disparate buildings. These include the Relief Congregation Church (on the left), which was established in 1828 and nearly a century later, in 1917, became the Pavilion Cinema, renamed the Dean Picture House in 1930. Nearby, a door pediment reads 'Dean Street UF Church Mission Hall 1884'. Raeburn Place was built between 1814 and 1825, with several villas on each side of the road. Some of these are still clearly visible as private houses behind the shop frontages built in the front garden ground of the original properties. The shop shown in the photograph between Dean Street and Raeburn Place is selling whisky, wines, spirits and pale ale.

Opposite: Hermitage Place in Stockbridge was renamed Raeburn Street in 1968 to avoid confusion with the other Hermitage Place in Leith. It runs from Dean Street to Raeburn Place and is shown on Kirkwood's map of 1817 with access from Dean Street only. The two-storey terraced houses, built on the west side only, were constructed between 1816 and 1819. On the right of the picture, a gate pillar can be seen with the iron fixings for a set of gates which were once closed at night.

Raeburn Place is the main road running west from Stockbridge to Comely Bank and on to South Queensferry. The thoroughfare slowly came to prominence after the first stone bridge was built over the Water of Leith in 1786. Even by 1817, however, Kirkwood's map shows development westwards of the bridge for only a few hundred yards on both sides of the road. Mary's Place is shown as a secondary name on the south side. Raeburn Place and Street take their name from Sir Henry Raeburn, Scotland's foremost portrait painter. Raeburn was born on 4 March 1756 in a modest cottage in Stockbridge, the younger son of William Raeburn, a yarn-boiler. Having lost both parents by the time he was six years old, he was educated at Heriot's Hospital and later apprenticed to James Gilliland, the goldsmith. After studying art in London and Rome he returned to Edinburgh and set up his studio in George Street in 1787, moving to York Place in 1795. This early twentieth century view looks east along Raeburn Place to the centre of Stockbridge. By that time Victorian tenements lined the street and many of the original villas had been spoiled by the addition of shops in their front gardens.

St Stephen's United Free Church was erected on the corner of Comely Bank Road and East Fettes Avenue in 1901. The design, by J. N. Scott and A. Lorne Campbell in red sandstone, included a tower and spire, but these were never built (the base of the intended tower can be seen to the left of the church noticeboard). The congregation can trace its history to 1844 when proposals for a Free Church in Stockbridge were first mooted. Of much less significance, but interesting nonetheless, is the small timber shelter on the left, originally used as a cabbie's hut.

This postcard was sent by 'AMD' to a Miss Leslie of Kingussie on 26 October 1908. The message on the card reads: 'Here are seven bonnie posties all in a row, but the one that you love best is not there, but here's from the one that you know, x'. Comely Bank Post Office, at 10 Comely Bank Avenue, was run by the Misses J. & M. Glen whose names are on the front window. There is an advertisement above the door for Paton's Alloa knitting wools, as well as a post office notice which lists the classes of business transacted: money order, savings bank, parcel post, insurance and annuity.

Comely Bank, Edinburgh.

This view looks westwards from outside St Stephen's United Free Church (seen on the previous page). The opening on the right is East Fettes Avenue, while on the left is a branch of Macvitties, Guest & Co., the bakers, who had numerous shops throughout Edinburgh. The parked lorry belongs to John Bruce & Son, wholesale egg merchants of 70 Montgomery Street, Edinburgh. In 1931 their telegraph address was, appropriately, 'hen'.

An Edinburgh & District Tramways Company cable car at the Comely Bank terminus, probably in August 1916. The board on the front of the car reads 'Albert Hall Picture Palace, twice nightly matinee every Saturday'. The other advertisements on the windows are less distinct but can be made out as: left window, 'Fun Fair and Carnival at Saughton Games Park, 7 August' and on the right window two features for the Palace Cinema: *Strength* and *Outwitted by the Maid. Courtesy of A. W. Brotchie Collection.*

This view of St Bernard's Well looks downstream to St Bernard's Bridge, which carries India Place across the Water of Leith. Lord Gardenstone, a senator of the College of Justice, believing that he had benefited from the medicinal properties of the Water of Leith, commissioned Alexander Naysmith in 1788 to build the present well on the site of a much smaller structure. The domed roof is supported by ten plain Doric columns, within which stands a statue of Hygeia. The original statue was replaced by one carved by D. W. Stevenson when the well was refurbished by William Nelson, the printer, around 1887. Beside the well, on its east side, a stone tablet encircles a low relief medallion of Nelson by the sculptor John Rhind. Above it are the words: THE LIBERAL DEVISETH LIBERAL THINGS, and the entwined initials W. N.